Taking Flight

by Adriana Sevahn Nichols

A SAMUEL FRENCH ACTING EDITION

SAMUEL FRENCH

FOUNDED 1830

NEW YORK HOLLYWOOD LONDON TORONTO

SAMUELFRENCH.COM

ISBN 978-0-573-69616-9   Printed in U.S.A.   #22323

MUSIC USE NOTE

IMPORTANT BILLING AND CREDIT
REQUIREMENTS

All producers of *TAKING FLIGHT* must give credit to the Author of the Play in all programs distributed in connection with performances of the Play, and in all instances in which the title of the Play appears for the purposes of advertising, publicizing or otherwise exploiting the Play and/or a production. The name of the Author *must* appear on a separate line on which no other name appears, immediately following the title and *must* appear in size of type not less than fifty percent of the size of the title type.

In addition the following credit *must* be given in all programs and publicity information distributed in association with this piece:

TAKING FLIGHT was developed and first produced by Center Theatre Group/Kirk Douglas Theatre in the Festival SOLOMANIA 2006 Michael Ritchie, Artistic Director; Charles Dillingham, Managing Director "Developed with Assistance of the Sundance Institute" 2004 HPP Festival at South Coast Repertory

TAKING FLIGHT was first produced by the Center Theatre Group in Los Angeles on May 14, 2006. The play was written and performed by Adriana Sevahn Nichols.

The performance was directed by Giovanna Sardelli, with sets by Edward E. Haynes, Jr., costumes by Candice Cain, lighting by José López, percussion by Michito Sanchez, sound design by Adam Phalen, and video by Daniel Foster/EyeAwake Studios. The Production Stage Manager was Scott Harrison.

PLAYWRIGHT'S TECHNICAL NOTES

The overall tone of this play, technically, should be very simple.

The entire play is performed by one actor.

The only set pieces/props that are essential are a chair, live white flowers, a bowl or vessel to float the flowers in, and a black cardigan sweater. Fake flowers should not be substituted as they are an offering to the goddess, Yemaya. Even one live beautiful white flower will do.

The lighting should be magical, transporting us from location to location, easily, depicting the stark fluorescent sterility of the hospital, to the eerie apocalyptic New York streets, to the warmth of the flashback memories, to the "Vegas/magenta/mambo/magic" world of Esperanza.

The Rumi poem should be displayed somehow during the pre-show cue and become prominent as the house lights are going down, prior to the start of dialogue.

When there is an actress, other than Adriana Sevahn Nichols, performing the play, please substitute all references to Adriana with the real first name of the actress. It is important that she feel herself inside this story.

PLAYWRIGHT TO STORYTELLER

The overall pace of the story is mercurial. It is important that the storytelling stay ahead of the audience. The transitions between scenes and the transformations, in and out of each character, therefore, need to be seamless. Explore having the end of one character's gesture become the beginning of the next character's gesture. The more specific you make each vocal and physical choice, for each character, the more grounded and free you will feel as storyteller.

I invite you to use the audience. Make generous contact with them. Dare to see them and feel them. Allow yourself to need them as your confidant, witness, and trusted companion. I have found that it is a gift every time I have told this story. It is also a responsibility. We are asking the audience go on a deep journey of the heart with us, so as storyteller, it is essential not to indulge our emotions. We will certainly feel them, but if we give into them, we risk the audience feeling unsafe. And finally, play the heck out of the comedy, for therein lies the magic!

ACKNOWLEDGEMENTS

When I began writing for the theatre in 2002, I thought that playwriting was a solitary act. I now know it takes a village. Here's to the most amazing village a girl could ever ask for:

My love and deepest thanks to...

My Mom for encouraging me always to live my dreams and to be inspired, not defeated, by a closed door. My Dad for his passion. My Abuela for her example of how to live with unshakable faith, walk with the santos, and be juicy at 90. Giovanna Sardelli, my friend and director, your faith in me before a word was ever written, made the impossible, possible. Angel David, INTAR, and all who participated in 9/11 Writers Respond 2002. Diane Rodriquez (fairy goddess mother of this play), Robert Castro, John Glore, Jessica Goldberg, Gloria Calderon Kellett, Leilani Chan, Eileen Galindo, TeAda Productions, and all of the women in the '04 Latino Theatre Initiative's Women's Writing Retreat at the Mark Taper Forum. The direction of Tony Plana, Suzanne Karpinski, Juliette Carrillo, Jerry Patch, Jennifer Kieger, and all who participated in the '04 HPP at South Coast Rep. Tony your generous gift of time and creative genius at SCR and Rio Hondo College transformed TAKING FLIGHT from a memory monologue into a play. Ivonne Coll, Leo Garcia, and Jen Cleary at Highways Theatre. Philip Himberg, Deborah Stover, the brilliant Mame Hunt, Meredith Lynsey Schade, Larry Cesspooch, my fellow colleagues, the waterfall, and all of nature's spirits in abundance at the '05 Sundance Theatre Lab. Michael Ritchie, Kelly Kirkpatrick, Pier Carlo Talenti, David Franklin, Scott Harrison, Jose Lopez, Adam Phalen, Ed Haynes, Michito Sanchez, Daniel Foster, Candace Cain, Kenny Wurther, the guys of SOLOMANIA, the entire CTG family, Kirk and Anne Douglas, and the Culver City Fire Department. Dr. Bert Mandelbaum, Kerri Campbell, and the amazing donor who gave me his ACL, it is because of all of you that I can dance, again. Susan Loewenberg, wise director Stuart K. Robinson, luminous composer Chaundra Cogburn, goddess music supervisor Allison Clarke, musicians Gooding, Joseph Julian Gonzales, Bruno Coon, Music Express, singers Marissa Steingold, from the Agape Choir: Marianne Lewis, Ian Cousineau, Ken Thomas, Elijah Rock, angel Susan Raab, Mark Ward, Mark Holden, Patrick Morrison, and the entire LA Theatre Works family. The Durfee Foundation and the Spencer Cherashore Fund. Sam Woodhouse, John Anderson, Victoria Petrovich, Tom Jones, Chelsea Kashin, and the entire San Diego Rep family. Anahid Sharik, Karen Kondazian, Simon Levy, Stephen Sachs, Deborah Lawson, Christian Epps, Scott Tuomey, and the Fountain Theatre family. The amazing Gardner House Girls. Henry Godinez, Roche Schulfer, John Collins, and the entire Goodman Theatre family. And to the magic makers, who have inspired me to love, to live, and to fly, my sweetheart Jonathan Nichols, my incredible agent Antje Oegel, my teachers Omar Shapli, Robbie McCauley, Laurie Carlos, Kristen Linklater, Fran Bennett, Carol Gilligan, Peter Loffredo, Master Kim, Satyan and Suzanne Raja, Stephen Garrett, Nilo Cruz, my soul friends Richard Greene and Lynn Milgrim, my sweet girls Maggie and Luna, and to the goddesses Marissa Chibas, Onahoua Rodriguez, Emunah, Anna, Sunny, Allana, Jennifer, Michelle, and Veronica.

–Adriana Sevahn Nichols

I dedicate TAKING FLIGHT to...
Peter Loffredo for showing me the path,
John Leguizamo for illuminating it,
and to my beloved, Jonathan, for crawling,
walking, and dancing with me,
every step of the way.

PROLOGUE

(A Rumi Poem is to be displayed/projected somewhere, on the set, during pre-show look that is visible to the audience:)

The way of love is not
a subtle argument.

The door there
is devastation.

Birds make great sky circles
of their freedom.

How do they learn it?

They fall, and falling,
they are given wings.

–Rumi

(As house lights fade, the poem should be prominently lit, cross fading into start of show...)

(...ADRIANA enters the stage carrying the bud of a live white rose. She regards the audience. She offers a silent prayer as she places the open blossom into a bowl of water. She walks in a circle around the playing area, arms outstretched, preparing the space. When complete, she reaches into the bowl of water and gathers some in her hands. She throws it onto the circle. Lights shift. The circle is alive. She enters it.)

ADRIANA. *(on her cell phone)* Hey Rhonda it's me. Listen, I'm running late. I just got out of the workshop. The Introduction to the Shamanic Journey workshop at the Open Center?! Hold on. *(She addresses the audience directly.)* I'm so sorry. I just had to make this call. I'll be right with all of you.

(Back to RHONDA.)

Rhonda, it was amazing. This guy, his name is Machete, El Gran Shaman of Peru. I mean I called him Bird-man, because his spirit animals are like the Condor and all of the sacred birds of the Mayans...or was it the Incans? Anyway – no, listen, so all of these freaks are there, right? Like total losers. Quasi-spiritually wounded children types. They all circle around him like he's some freakin' rock star, but me wise woman in waiting...I hold back. I wait until every last groupie had groped him for a blessing. And Rhonda, when I looked into his eyes, I knew, that he knew, that I KNOW!

What? I thought your fitting was next Thursday? Well, we'll figure it out later – listen, listen! I bought this really amazing gourd rattle – it's to call in the spirits – I can't wait to show you. And sweetie, Birdman and I know each other from *before.* I'm getting its somewhere between my lifetime as the priestess of Athena and the beheading in France. Oh! I saw this flyer for this work-shop, it's called, "Celebrating the Goddess Within," we have to go! I think it would be great for you to do this workshop before you get married. I don't know...we'll dance, we'll sing, we'll eat chocolate. It'll be great!

What? I thought you were going with purple and mauves?

(Covering the phone, she whispers to audience.) I'm so sorry she talks so much.

(back to **RHONDA***)* I don't know. I'll have to see it – look I'm hopping on the train right now. Ok. I love you too. Bye. *(She hangs up.)*

(to audience)

My best friend Rhonda and I are planning her wedding for next fall and she is driving me crazy talking endlessly about the minutia of every last detail, every day. The day Brian and I get married, it will be by a mountain stream or on a beach somewhere – you know…simple…home-cooked…a handful of special people. Not Rhonda. So far her guest list is pushing two hundred and that's small to her.

*(***RHONDA*** speaks with a very heavy Long Island "Jewish-American Priestess" accent. Her laugh is deliciously annoying and reminiscent of Fran Dresher and a blender crushing ice.)*

RHONDA. Honey, you remember how I told you my dream was to get married in the Italian countryside? Well it's going to come true. Mike and I just found the place.

ADRIANA. Oh. That's great.*(to audience)* Shit. I have already been feeling stressed out about financing the bridesmaid dress I will never wear again and the expensive gift I'll have to give them. I mean Rhonda has always been so generous to me and now a ticket to Italy?

RHONDA. Are you ready for this? We just found a little fake Tuscan villa, on a vineyard, right out on the tip of Long Island.

ADRIANA. *(whispers to audience)* Thank God!

RHONDA. And, in the middle of all those grapes, it came to me. I'm gonna have gold, crimson, and burnt orange decorations. A *harvest* theme. And I'm gonna walk down that aisle in an apricot colored taffeta Vera Wang with hair extensions down to my waist. *(laughs)*

ADRIANA. Okaaay...It's starting to sound like the Godfather meets the Mists of Avalon.

RHONDA. Oh shut up. I'm not done yet! So, what was my second dream???

ADRIANA. *(unenthusiastically)* To have Bon Jovi play at your wedding – OH MY GOD! You got Bon Jovi to play your wedding?

RHONDA. No Einstein, but I got the best Bon Jovi cover band on Long Island to play for the ceremony, and they gave me a great deal cuz I told them I have hot lookin' bridesmaids in corsets and they could stay for the party!

ADRIANA. Great. So I'm gonna have a drunk Bon Jovi wannabe waiting for my tits to pop out of my dress?

RHONDA. Don't worry Brian will give him that icy Nordic stare of his and scare him off.

ADRIANA. What about the Klezmer band your parents hired?

RHONDA. I'm putting them outside the bathroom. Now shush...sit down. I worked out the opening, I want you to see it, and then you can show me your magic gourd.

(We hear the dramatic opening of a rock n' roll Bach Fugue which sounds something like the opening to Bon Jovi's "Let it Rock." **RHONDA** speaks over the music. She paints each image as the musical interludes accompany her epic plan.)*

Ok...The iron gates to the vineyard fly open...this is where you guys start filing in down the aisle. Brides-maids...Bridesmaids...Bridesmaids...Bridesmaids... My little cousin with the flower petals. Now...silence... I enter...everyone sees my dress. I look gorgeous. I look at my Father. I take my Father's arm. *(beat)* Ok, I don't know what do with this part. I was hoping you could help me. But when Bon Jovi starts singin', that's when I'm gonna start walking down the aisle towards Mike. You ready?

*See Music Use Note on Page 3.

(RHONDA gives herself space to walk down the aisle.)

Oh my God, what are you cryin' for already? She's so dramatic! Aaaannd…

(As the electric guitar plays a march-like rhythm, RHONDA does a rock n' roll walk down the aisle.)

What do you think?

(Phone rings. Music stops as lights shift.)

ADRIANA. Hello? Mike! Oh my god! I told you she was. Where is she? What? Uh-huh…Uh-huh…What does that mean? Do you think she's going to make it? She did? No, I'll be there…I don't know…but you tell her I'll be there…I will…you too…

(She hangs up the phone. She dials frantically.)

They found Rhonda. Yeah. No, it's not good. She's in ICU. Mike just called. The doctors are saying they don't know if she's going to make it and he said that she was asking for me, so…I wanted to ask if you'll go to the hospital with – No, I can't ask Brian. He's home, but I can't ask. No, its ok, I understand. You too –

(She hangs up. Back to audience.)

I call three other people before I finally reach Gabriella, a mutual friend of mine and Rhonda's. She is my last hope, so when she says, "I'll go to the hospital with you even though Rhonda didn't ask for me," I am so relieved. Gabi is a champion synchronized swimmer and she sees everything as a competition, which can be so exhausting, but I appreciate her honesty and I am grateful not to have to go alone. I have no idea how the hell I'm going to get down there and I don't know what the hell to wear. I mean what do you wear to maybe say goodbye? Do you get dressed up? After all, Rhonda is the high priestess of the fashion police. No! That's ridiculous. I'm going to wear a grey t–shirt, an old pair of jeans, no make–up, my hair pulled back… that seems respectful. I'll try and get a cab to 14th Street and then pray for a miracle. I take my Grandmother's rosary beads with me, just in case.

(Takes rosary beads from a small altar. She holds them as she prays…)

Abuela. Por favor. Cuidame a Rhonda. La queiro ver. Y ayudame a llegar al hospital. Te queiro tanto. Gracias.

(Lights shift to a tight special. Inside the cab. She speaks to the audience.)

The cab driver looks at me intently through the rear view mirror. I cry most of the drive. I tell him the little I know about Rhonda's condition. It helps me to keep talking. He shakes his head…and he says…

CABBIE. *(In a heavy Haitian accent)* You know what scare me now…dis enemy…is like a ghost…ya don see…you can't see…so who do you trust?

ADRIANA. I notice the tiny brand new American flag he has taped to the meter. It's around 9 pm when he drops me off. He won't take any money for the fare, not even a tip, he says,

CABBIE. Dat what you tole me Miss, break my heart. But I gon' pray for you and your friend.

(Lights shift)

ADRIANA. I start trying to convince the cops on York Avenue to let me cross the barricade.

ADRIANA. Excuse me officer, my friend is in ICU and –

COP #1. *(Heavy NY accent)* Only residents with the proper ID, M'am, next –

ADRIANA. First Avenue…Officer my friend is in ICU and she's –

COP #2. *(African–American.)* I'm sorry Ma'am it's just too dangerous, I can't let you by here, next –

ADRIANA. Second Avenue…Officer please –

COP #3. *(Irate New York accent)* I'm not tellin' you people again – now back it up!

ADRIANA. I am now a wreck on Third Avenue. I march right up to the Highway Patrol Cop with the kind eyes… "Please Officer, my friend is in ICU – I gotta get down there – she's asking for me and she may not make it through the ni – " He puts his hand on my shoulder and he tears up. I knew I had found my man, or maybe the cabbie had just started praying…

(She crosses through the barricade.)

My cop with the kind eyes starts flagging down every vehicle allowed past the barricade, but no one will take me. Finally, this tiny blue Honda civic pulls up with a tired looking doctor still in his stethoscope, scrubs, and clogs. He agrees to take me. I tell him about Rhonda's condition and ask him if there is any way he thinks she can survive…the deep breath he takes before he answers…tells me no. When we get within a few blocks of the hospital. Cops yell at us to get out of the car. No private vehicles allowed past the checkpoint. But I don't want to get out of the car alone – thankfully my doctor, Dr. Earl Noilan, says he'll walk with me.

(Lights shift. It is dark. There is a faint sound of a gritty wind and distant siren that penetrate the eerie silence. She moves slowly.)

We get out of the car. I can't see. The black smoke is so thick I can't see the names of the streets. My lungs feel as if they are being squeezed. I can't get any air. We move slowly…feeling what we can't see…I begin to feel nauseous…from the smell…the horrible smell that I taste in my mouth. We are lost in a labyrinth of streets. I can't breathe…my chest hurts…then I remember… I have a doctor next to me…so I ask him if it would be ok if I hold his hand…and he says of course and reaches his warm hand out to me.

(Lights shift.)

We turn the corner and we are blinded by an apocalyptic veil of white light and there in the midst of this eerie cloud is the front entrance to the hospital. It looks like the set of a movie…like maybe some TV show had lent the hospital those big lights they use for the night shoots. The entrance is shrouded in an endless wallpaper of missing people flyers…fluttering smiles…last seen…last wearing…

Mike is standing out front and Gabi is right there next to him. I hug my doctor goodbye and as I watch his green form re-enter the dark ash, I think...I should bake him some cookies.

Well Gabi is wearing her sexy ivory colored sundress and make-up and of course I immediately feel underdressed.

(They enter the hospital.)

It's hard to believe that 12 hours ago this place was a major medical center. Now, the entire hospital is running on a generator, no lights or A/C in nonessential areas. The phones are dead. And outside every window is the relentless blizzard of black ash. We stop briefly in the bathroom on the first floor to collect ourselves.

ADRIANA. *(fixing her hair in the mirror)* Should we say a prayer?

GABRIELLA. Here in the bathroom?

*(**ADRIANA** nods.)*

GABRIELLA. *(tentatively)* Ok.

(They take hands.)

ADRIANA. Great Spirit...Abeula...and all those that watch over us. Thank you for getting us here safely. Thank you for taking care of Rhonda today. Please keep her safe from...*(The prayer becomes inaudible while **ADRIANA** continues and the sound of a toilet flushing loud and long drowns out her voice.)* and help us to know what...*(flushing toilet again)...(after toilet gurgles settle)*...thank you.

GABRIELLA. That was beautiful.

ADRIANA. Thanks. You ready?

(To audience) We take the dark stairs up to room 302.

(A lone sound of a heart monitor beeping.)

We enter Rhonda's room...quietly.

*(**ADRIANA** crosses to center where the chair is placed with the black sweater over the back. This will become the hospital room and bed whenever referred to as such.)*

She looks beautiful. I am so relieved to see that her face has been untouched. It's hard to get close to her because of all of the equipment around her. Her heart monitor starts racing when she sees us. She struggles to speak around the respirator tube in her mouth...

RHONDA. *(heavily drugged)* I'm so fucked up...I'm so fucked up.

ADRIANA. Gabi and I stand on either side of her bed side, holding both of her hands, like two bookends, not knowing what to do. Rhonda can't take her eyes off of Gabi, she looks so luminous in her sundress.

RHONDA. *(struggles to speak)* Oh Gabi you...Goddess...

ADRIANA. *(to audience)* Shit hello? I dress down out of respect and I am virtually invisible.

RHONDA. Oh...Yemaya...

(Lights shift. We hear soft ocean waves. **RHONDA** *rises out of the chair and comes forward. She is completely healthy and strong as she embodies this memory. This will be true of all flashbacks.)*

RHONDA. Adriana and I were goin' on this retreat called, "Celebrating the Goddess Within," and part of our homework was ta choose a goddess and start a relationship with her. So I didn't know what goddess ta pick. And I was talkin' ta Adriana about it, so she asks me, "What do I love most in nature?" So I tell ha, I love the sea. I'm from Oyster Bay, Long Island and I've always loved the ocean. So she starts tellin' me about this goddess that her Grandmother used to pray to called, Yemaya. So Adriana takes me up to this place called a Botanica. *(She laughs.)* We walk in and there's this weird lookin' creature behind the door – well I mean it wasn't alive or anything, but like this figure, made out of wood with coconuts all around it and pennies and candles – black candles – which made me a little uncomfortable. It was a teeny tiny little place, but there was all this stuff for the money, the health, the good luck – it all felt a little hokey to me, you know, like a lot a voo doo tschotchkas, but then we got to this section where they had all of this stuff for Yemaya, the goddess of the sea...

(We hear a soft sensual drumbeat...magic enters the story.)

...and she is so beautiful. She has this really long dark hair and it looks like she has a bit of a tan. She's in this beautiful flowing white dress, nice figure, and her arms are open like...like she was calling me and when I looked at her I felt such peace, that I knew I had found my Goddess. *(Drumbeat ends.)*

So I got a Yemaya candle. A royal blue one to bring with me on the retreat. And they put some silver sparkles on it – I could choose between silver and gold – I chose the silver because I did not think the gold matched Yemaya's outfit. Adriana had chosen the goddess, Oya *(She laughs.)* Oyaaaaa! I couldn't resist asking if she was the goddess from Minnesota? So Adriana looks at me real serious like she does sometimes and she goes, "No. Oya is the goddess of the wind and the cemeteries. She's a warrior goddess symbolizing female power, righteous anger, and the storms of change!" You know Adriana can be so dramatic sometimes. So I said well ok, honey, that sounds festive. So she got her burgundy colored candle with everything on it and off we went – laughing and walkin' arm in arm down Amsterdam Ave. Oh!! They were filming *Law & Order* on the corner and we were trying to see Jesse Martin. I think he's so cute. And I was tellin' Adriana, "See, she shoulda been carrying around her headshots!" Cuz, I mean you never know, that coulda been a great opportunity for her. We really had fun that day...the day I fell in love with Yemaya, the goddess of the sea.

(We hear the return of the ocean waves. **RHONDA** *recedes back into the chair. She takes two slow deep breaths. Her heart monitor starts beeping again.)*

ADRIANA. The nurses are busy, checking and filling, checking and emptying and occasionally smiling softly at us. Rhonda is covered from her chest to her feet in a stiff white sheet. Now, Gabi had already warned me that she gets faint at the sight of blood and yet I know that we both want to see what the hell happened to our friend. We don't want to wake her, or hurt her, so very gently we begin sliding the sheet up. Rhonda's toes poke out at us still sporting the Black Cherry Pedicure she had gotten with me at the Pinky nail salon on Broadway *(nervous giggles)*…we continue pulling the sheet up –
Rhonda fades back into consciousness, she pulls the entire sheet back with a grand flourish, and says that she wants us to see her. Gabi nearly hits the floor, as she whispers, "That she'll be right baaaack."

(beat)

So there I am, alone, with Rhonda. I look down at her mangled body. It looks like she's been turned inside out. She is lying in a pool of blood soaked bandages. Her legs from the knees down have been ground up like meat and what is left of them is being held together with thick steel rods and screws. Parts of her have been sewn closed like a rag doll with thick black thread and staples and from the side I can see the skin from her upper back is missing and is a gaping hole. I stare…not recognizing her body…one that I know so well. Holding the sheet up she says,

RHONDA. See…see what happened?

ADRIANA. Like a little kid that can't wait to show you her boo-boo. And I say…
I see you. I see you.

*(We hear the pulsing of a delicious Mambo beat, and are jolted by the heat of fabulous magenta lights. **ESPERANZA**, born out of the depth of this pain, explodes into the room. She is a cross between Carmen Miranda and Doctor Phil "in the hood." She takes us to a realm of the goddess and Caribbean magic. She may not have the budget of Celine Dion, but when you're the real thing baby, who needs it!)*

ESPERANZA. Good Evening Ladies and Gentleman!
I am Esperanza an I will bring you hope
I will take away jour pain and then ju and I will smoke!

Whepa!!!

I am the life of the party of life!
Oh jes, I an the real thing baby.
No crazy Birdman from Peru. *(She makes fun of him with a bird call.)*

Pleassse!

I am Espereranza Middleschmerz
A crazy name
I know

Ju ask why?
Bueno ju didn't ask why
Pero theatrically I say why
So we can keep this going
Because ju people are berry berry quiet.

So you ask why?
I tell ju

Because I believe that without hope
there is no heart
an without heart
there is no life
so I an hope
ju know?!

An then Middleschmerz
That's berry berry creative.

(She addresses a man in the audience.)

Ay papi, ju look confuse
mira, Middleschmerz is the pain that the womans hab
in the middle of the month
An that's why...

I am the hope

in the middle
of the pain!

Whepa!

Ok Adrianita, listen to me berry carefully...dis is what
you hab been waiting for your entire co-dependant
life. This is the big Kahuna. Are ju ready Mamita becuz
we hab work to do!

(We hear the pulse of Afro Cuban drums. **ESPERANZA**
*smells the air...obviously she is in her element...the dark-
ness is no match for her.)*

Shhh! We hab to clean this room because this air is
full of death. Ssssssut. Ay un muerto aqui, un espiritu
atrasao, an we habs to get him out. Ahhhaa...don
thinks ju can hide from me ju hungry ghost. Ju will not
take this buriful girl with ju!

(She speaks to **ADRIANA**.*)*

Oye Nena muevate we don't hab time! Look if ju jus
going to stand there then get out of my way because I
hab a life to save.

(Goes to the head of **RHONDA**'s *bed.)*

Ay Dios mio, mi cielo, dis bed is facing west! I'm going
to turn ju to the morning light...so much darkness...
we need light!

Adriana take this stalk of yerba buena and Florida
water and I want ju to beat the darkness out of this
floor. *(shows her how)* Clean. Everything must be clean.
Because the devil hides in corners and under the dust
of all the peoples that came here to die.

Hand me my cigar and my botella de rum...

Ay Maria Santisima y en el gran nobre de Jesus
Ayudame mis Santos a salvar esta pobre muchacha...

*(***ESPERANZA**'s *body shakes as she becomes possessed with
the Holy spirit. She circles the bed in a rhythmic Afro-
Cuban dance to cleanse the room. She alternates between
puffing cigar smoke and spraying rum, through her
mouth, onto* **RHONDA**, *after each line.)*

Que se vaya de aqui todo los espiritus atrassado.....
huhhhh

y la echiseria...huuuh

y la macumba...huhhh !!!!

(Her dance builds to a fever pitch as she battles with the dark spirits until she is satisfied that **RHONDA** *is safe. She stops in a grand and abrupt gesture and addresses the audience... out of breath...)*

Ay People, I am getting too old for dis. I need a little refreshments. A little Pina Colada. *(She sips water.)* Bacardi 151 baby! Ayyyy yai yai yaiiii! *(She holds her forehead.)* I got, how ju call it, a little brain freeze!

Ok, where was I...Aqui!

(ESPERANZA *stands behind* **RHONDA**'s *chair, like a guardian, as she prays over her.)*

Yemaya...madre de los mares...lady of the moon...protect your daughter...Rhonda...she needs ju now. Send los angelitos of light to surround this child of jours and keep her safe from di dark spirits that try to take her today.

(ESPERANZA *sings praise to Yemaya.)* Yemaya oro mi nee a ye o...Yemaya!

(ADRIANA *puts her hand in the vessel of water and offers it to the Goddess...she whispers...)*

Hekua Yemaya...Hekua....

(Lights shift. Sound of heart monitor beeping.)

ADRIANA. It's Rhonda's third night in ICU. I wash my hands before making my way to her bedside. Since the slightest infection could kill her, it's a rule that everyone has to wash their hands upon entering her room. There's a little sink with a sign above it that says "quiet healing in progress." We are also supposed to wear gloves, but I don't because Rhonda hates how they feel, so I make sure that my hands are immaculate before I touch her. I stare at her as she sleeps. Her body trembles softly. She still has the respirator tube stuffed down her throat, IV poles everywhere, monitors beeping.....

Her bed is made of sand and it looks like a big blue inflatable boat that you'd pile into on a cool summer lake. It keeps rippling quiet waves underneath her so she won't have any pressure on her wounds and with her mane of crimson colored curls cascading all around her, she looks like a mermaid taking a rest on a floating island.

(Lights shift. Flashback. We hear a cacophony of gongs and chants in woman's voice.)

ADRIANA. *(chants...uninspired)*

Earth my body

Water my blood

Air my breath

And fire my spirit

We are at the, "Celebrating the Goddess Within" weekend retreat. It is Saturday afternoon already and I am wondering when the hell we are going to get to the "celebrating" part? We're all sitting around in this circle grabbing the stupid talking stick, that's the thing with the feathers that's supposed to make you tell the truth, and the women are moaning, "I feel...I feel..." Oh my God, if I have to listen to another story about somebody's horrible abuse, or neglect, I am going to lose my mind. I can't believe Rhonda and I payed good money for this. Look, I love putting on the really fun goddessy kinda clothes and the jewelry and sitting around eating delicious meals that we all help each other cook, and getting the sleepover giggles in the tents–like that part is fun...but then why the hell don't we just go camping and cut out all the psycho crap?

Anyway...we're sitting around the circle and for some reason none of us notice that Rhonda is missing.

All of a sudden we hear this laughter coming from outside the door and we're all like, "What the hell is going on?" Rhonda bursts into the room and she howls... "huuhhuuaaaaahuuaaaa!"...she is stark naked.... dripping wet...looking gorgeous...and she like...

RHONDA. Oh my God you guys. Oh my God. I went into the pond. I just jumped into the pond. It is so gorgeous in there. You have to come. You have to come. Just come on!

ADRIANA. So we look at our "group leader" and she's like go! Go! Thank God. Free from that stupid circle. *(re-enacting the entire scene)* We strip off our clothes and we run down like crazy ninnies to this freezing cold pond…Rhonda leading the way…her big titties flappin in the breeze…I'm screaming…

"I'm not doing this Rhonda. I have Dominican blood in me. I hate cold water. You understand? I take hot baths, hot showers. I swim in warm oceans. No no no no no!"

RHONDA. Oh c'mon Adriana, you're gonna love it. You're gonna love it. Cmon.!

ADRIANA. No Rhonda, I can't, it's too cold. It's too cold.

RHONDA. Cmon Adriana. Cmon. Take my hand. Count of three. Here we go. Cmon. 1.2.3.

AAiiiiihhhhhhhhhhhhhhhiiieeeeeeeee!

(Holding hands they jump into the pond's icy depths.)

ADRIANA. *(gasping and shivering)* Oh my God.

RHONDA. Isn't it gorgeous?! Isn't it wonderful?! C'mon, fix your hair honey. Fix your hair. *(She throws her head back, into water, holding her nose.)*

ADRIANA. *(She repeats motion, shivering through blue lips.)* Uh huh huh huh…huh…Oh it is uhhh beautiful…. urrrrr…in…here. Oooooowhoooo….the sun…. is uhhhh…just like….so beautiful. Okay, I'm getting out……it's just too cold!!!

RHONDA. Oh you're a wuss!

ADRIANA. *(To audience)* Rhonda is just swimming around like a fish in there. I can hardly believe it…I mean she's scared of so many other things, but to see her swimming in that water, just like a mermaid…

*(Sound of beautiful melody as we see **RHONDA** embody*

*this moment of freedom and beauty. Heart monitor fades
back in as* **ADRIANA***'s memory recedes. She returns to*
RHONDA*'s bedside.*)

The ICU nurse comes in to check Rhonda's vital signs
every 10 minutes. They've been doing this for the past
three days. Her doctors are worried. She has a severe
infection. Her temperature has spiked up to 103, so
they are keeping a close watch.

(beat)

I decided not to make the same mistake of dressing
down again because Rhonda has no memory of me
being there that first night, but she has total recall
of *Goddess Gabriella* in her flowing white dress. So I
am wearing an *unforgettable* magenta sari and a lapis
moonstone necklace. Rhonda startles me as she snaps
back into consciousness, and grabs hold of my sari...
"Honey...hi...what is it...are you in pain...what do you
need...oh God...let me go call the nurse?" She main-
tains her white-knuckled grip on the folds of my sari as
she pulls me close, and mouths...

RHONDA. *(with great effort)* Is that new?

(ADRIANA *nods.*)

RHONDA. You look...*beautiful....*

ADRIANA. And that was a glorious moment because it meant
our Rhonda was still here and Goddess Gabriella had
now been replaced by Goddess Adriana!

(Lights shift.)

My lack of wardrobe and fashion sense has always been
of great concern to Rhonda, she being the unparal-
leled high fashion priestess of the upper eastside. It
boggles my mind the way she puts things together. The
colors, the textures, the accessories. Jesus, I just grab
whatever is clean and I'm good to go. Not Rhonda.
She had a...*has*...a ritzy Wall St. job. She's an invest-
ment banker. She hates it, but her clothes habit makes
her a slave to it. But the best part is that whenever

she'd clean out her closets, which was often, she'd call me to come over and pick up a bag of goodies. This sweater was in the last bag she gave me.

(She takes the sweater off the back of the chair. She puts it on.)

I hate it. It's just not me. I remember how happy she was because...

RHONDA. ...it comes with a matching sleeveless shell and I think this J.Crew ensemble will be just perfect for your auditions.

ADRIANA. I don't wear corporate black sweater sets to auditions. Oh no! I wear a low cut v-neck with a miracle bra that cuts off my circulation for all those slutty puta calls I go on. Well whenever I had an audition, I'd run over to her place, the night before, to run lines. She loved helping me, she even gave me direction, but she hated all the ethnic crap I'd go out for. You know, the...

ADRIANA. *(cont.) (touching herself while gyrating:)* "Ay Papi you feel so good! Ay Dios mio. Dios mio!"

(sobbing widow:) or "I was afraid to call the police because I didn't have the papers."

(overworked pregnant mother of 12) or "Jose Miguel Felipe Ramirez Gonzales, sientate en esa mesa, y come t'el arroz con pollo. Cono!!!" *(She slaps the child.)*

Rhonda would say....

RHONDA. I don't get it. I just don't get it. You're so talented, why do you go out for all this garbage? You don't even look Latin to me. You should be lawyer on *Law & Order* or Sarah Jessica Parker's new best friend on *Sex and the City.*

(beat)

ADRIANA. Well, Rhonda has been wearing a hospital gown for the past month. She is still in ICU. Same room. Same bed. Her doctors have told her family that she probably won't be able to walk again, but they haven't told Rhonda that, they just keep saying they're doing their best to get her home by Thanksgiving.

Since her only accessory now is a plastic ID bracelet which reads September 11th 9:13am...whenever I go to visit, I like to bring beauty and fashion to her. I take great care in coordinating the clothes, the hair, the make up, the jewelry, the purse. As soon as I enter her room she says...

RHONDA. Come here let me see you...

ADRIANA. I walk towards her...slowly. Do a little turn followed by a shaky leg extension so she can see my shoes. She loves shoes! They're usually the same old shoes, but she always asks to see them and I always show her. I wait for her blessings...

RHONDA. Hair looks good...that new?

ADRIANA. She drinks me in with her eagle eye and in these moments we are far from room 302...

(We hear the beginning of a Bon Jovi song.*)

RHONDA. I love you, JON BON JOVI!!!!

ADRIANA. We are back in her living room on East 83rd ST, eating soy cheese doodles, and talking about sex....

*(**RHONDA** and **ADRIANA** sing the first verse in a ridiculous duet.)*

RHONDA. Ooohhh. I got a stitch. Keep dancing! I'm exhausted. Mike had me up all night. We did it three times! He's been takin' these zinc supplements. He's like a rock.

ADRIANA. Ok. I'm totally jealous. I can't even remember the last time Brian and I had sex. He's so tired from work. He comes home around midnight, and he's exhausted – Can you believe he actually said this to me the other day, "Well, you need to be more visually stimulating." What the hell does that mean!? Am I supposed to slink around all night in patent leather boots and a nurse's outfit waiting for him to get home? I don't think so! How about a little date, dinner, a present...it takes time for me to warm up.

**See Music Use Note on Page 3.

RHONDA. Well honey, you gotta speed things up a bit...you know...help the guy out. I know what your problem is. You gotta get over trying to have the ideal orgasm from the "Look Ma no hands" school already. So God put your love button a little too far North...what are you gonna do? You're gonna get a rocket pocket!

ADRIANA. A rocket pocket?

RHONDA. A rocket pocket! It's so small it fits in the palm of your hand. You just hold it there while he's doin his thing and...*zzzzz...zzzzz...zzzzzzz...* OH MY GOD!!! I got the website right here for you. It's called "Opening Pandora's Box." *(She laughs.)* And sweetie, you gotta mow the lawn, you know? Trim those hedges so Brian can find your garden of paradise. He's from a cold country. He's used to hairless women. I think you should surprise him. I'm telling you, he won't be able to keep his hands off you. I got it! Hold onto your labia minora honey cuz I'm taking you to get your first Brazilian Bikini wax, my treat, you're gonna hate me during but boy are you gonna love me after...*(She laughs.)*

(Lights shift back to ICU.)

RHONDA. *(semi-drugged)* My doctors scheduled the skin grafting surgery for next Monday, cuz Mike has the day off for Columbus Day. I was wondering if you could come too so he's not here alone.

ADRIANA. Sure sweetie. I'll just have to tell Brian we –

RHONDA. Oh my God...Brian?! Honey, I forgot. Oh my God...Why haven't you said anything? Is he alright?

ADRIANA. He's ok...he's ok. He was fifteen minutes late for work, so he got there right after the second plane hit. He saw a lot of – Are you sure you want to talk about this?

RHONDA. Yeah. I'm wanna know.

ADRIANA. Well, he was late for work, so he got there around 9:15, but the trains had stopped running to World Trade...they made them get off at Chambers Street. He saw the flames and this big hole and for some reason he just kept walking towards it, to work. He saw a lot of people jump or fall. Rhonda, he remembers what they were all wearing. Meanwhile I'm standing in the middle of the living room watching all of this on TV and the phone is dead. I couldn't stop shaking. I didn't know if he was alive. I didn't know if you were alive. I wanted to go down there but I didn't know what I'd do or how…I mean Giuliani said the city was in lock down…so I just starting praying. I promised that if he walked through that door, I was going to hold onto him and never let go. That I would marry him the next day…you know, forget the stupid wedding…just keep holding on. But when he walked through that door, he didn't want to be touched. He wouldn't eat or talk. He just sat in front of the TV in his dusty blue suit, watching the towers come down over and over. I spent the rest of the day calling all of the hospitals every fifteen minutes looking for you, until Mike called, nine hours later, and said they had found you.

RHONDA. I wish I could remember, but all I got is…pieces. I remember walkin' outta the train station on Court-landt Street. I was gonna stop at Borders to pick up an anniversary card for Mike. I crossed Church St. and I remember feeling the ground shake…I thought it was the subway…

(to audience)

ADRIANA. The man that found Rhonda would fill in the blanks. He tracked her down at the hospital. When I got him alone he told me…

(Lights shift.)

MAN. There were about 200 people in the street just screaming and running for cover from the hot metal… sheets of glass…concrete after the plane hit…debris is flying everywhere…and I see this beautiful redhead… long curly hair…runnin' next to me…I hear this loud crash and I turn around to make sure the redhead's ok…and I see her on the ground, half a block away. I run back…she's in pieces…her legs below the knees… corkscrewed and dangling…her whole back is open… there's so much blood…and she's still tryin' to get up…so I just tell her to "Stay still honey, stay still"…I take off my jacket and tie it around her to hold her together…then I cover her with my body so the stampede of people won't trample what is left of her, while I scream for help! This guy flags down an ambulance. They get the people outta there who aren't as injured, but she's in too many pieces to lift her onto the stretcher – she's bleeding out – we gotta get her outta there, so we grab a sheet and slide it under her and with great care, we load her onto that ambulance… such a beautiful girl…

(Lights shift. We hear an upbeat shopping samba.)

ADRIANA. *(enthusiastic)* Ok, ready to pack the bag of goodies for Rhonda's visit!

Skeleton and bat decals for the Halloween manicure.

Purple velvet headband with batwings.

Purple feather pom-pom magic wand and pen.

Purple and Green silk butterflies to hang over her bed.

Photos of trees and the ocean to create a view.

And a big picture of Yemaya……

I arrive at the hospital with my bag of treasures, dressed to the nines. It is a week before Halloween and perfect sweater weather. I am wearing the matching black J.Crew sweater set Rhonda had given me, a fabulous pair of Ann Taylor black pants…I splurged on, and my Franco Sarto calf length boots. Marshalls. I even put on full makeup and hairspray. It took me an hour and a half to get ready and I am already feeling a blister on my baby toe, but the look on Rhonda's face when I walk into the room is totally worth it….

RHONDA. *(on morphine…dreamy with energy)* C'mere let me see you. Oh honey. You look wonderful. *(She laughs.)* Stand on that chair. I want to see all of you. Hair looks good. Love the boots. I'm not crazy about the sweater though.

ADRIANA. Sweetie, you gave this to me.

RHONDA. I did? Well now I know why. Can you give me my water? Look at all this…Honey, thank you. It feels like my Birthday and Christmas and Chanukah and –

ADRIANA. Rhonda's nurse interrupts as she announces the arrival of some visitors. I like to call them "fringe friends"…you know…the ones that stroll in usually around a holiday with frozen smiles, presents, exciting updates, and leave thirty minutes later feeling oh so good about themselves for having stopped by. I stand by Rhonda's bedside like a sentinel enjoying how awkward and uncomfortable and useless they seem to feel. "Did you wash your hands?" I bark. "And make sure you put on the gloves." I move about the room anticipating Rhonda's *every* need, flaunting my *intimate* knowledge of her world. I confer with her nurses as though we are colleagues, and delight when the Fringes inevitably have to run off somewhere…Bye…

RHONDA. Goodbye. Tell me the truth Adriana do I look awful? My hair?

ADRIANA. No. And Madam today is your lucky day because I am going to wash and style your hair.

RHONDA. How are you gonna do that?

ADRIANA. Well…*(She looks around…improvising.)* I am going to tie this garbage bag around you like an enormous hood. And I'll use the pee pee pan to catch the water.

RHONDA. No. That's disgusting. Ow…wait….*(She pushes the morphine button.)*…Ow…Owww…*(Struggling to breathe.)* Owww…No…I told them…I need more fucking Morphine *(*RHONDA *screams in pain.)* Owww…No… Owwwww!!!

ADRIANA. Alarms start screeching around her. I'm afraid to leave her alone. I run to the door, "Nurse! Nurse, room 302!" A crowd of nurses rush into her room. They push me outside…

(Lights shift. We hear a strong Afro Cuban drumbeat… the rhythm sounds like a heartbeat.)

ESPERANZA. Ay Dios mio! Look who jus' arrive at Chez Esperanza's Beauty Salon?! It's Rhonda e-bri-body! Go Rhonda. Go Rhonda. Ay nena, ju looks like a self conscious Americano on a Caribbean cruise who hasn't had enough Pina Coladas to let the fuego out. Dale Mamaita, today is jour lucky day, because I am taking ju on an unforgettable trip. When ju leave here...ju going to be a new woman!

ADRIANA. Just give her more Morphine! They need her chart, she's had too much, they need her doctor, he's in surgery, they need to call the anesthesiologist, he's not here. More white coats running down the hall and she's still screaming.

ESPERANZA. I am going to wash and style jour hair because we know these crazy nurses don't know how to handle our kind of hair. Right? How's that water temperature?

RHONDA. I feel cold.

ADRIANA. My God. Will someone help her?

RHONDA. Can you see all the hair I've lost? Tell me the truth, Esperanza!

ESPERANZA. E'cu me. E'cu me. E'cu me! Ju hair is buriful. An judging from how often you hab to shave that little toto of jours, ju hab nothing to worry about! Ju see Mami, sontimes life take ju all the way back to the beginning to start again. Sontimes ju hab to let go of everything ju counted on...jour home...jour name... and even jour hair...an like a baby ju start again...

ADRIANA. Why is she so quiet? What's wrong?!

RHONDA. I like it here Esperanza. Can I stay?

ESPERANZA. No mi vida. But I'm going to put my homemade avocado con diet 7-UP special hair conditioner on ju, a secret recipe from my Abuelita, and I jus want ju to keeps breathing...that's it, Mamita...in... and...out...in...and...out...*(whispers)* Go Rhonda. Go Rhonda. *(We hear the heart monitor...lights shift back to ICU.)*

ADRIANA. When they finally let me back into her room… they say that I can only see her for a few minutes. But that it would do her good.

(Beat.)

I'm so afraid to leave. And I am afraid to go home.

(Lights shift.)

ADRIANA. It's Thanksgiving night and Brian is pissed at me because he says I didn't put enough thought into our Thanksgiving dinner, which is ridiculous since neither one of us likes turkey and we both agreed we weren't going to make a big fuss this year.

(The phone rings.)

ADRIANA. I'll get it.

(Answers phone) Hello.

RHONDA. *(Stronger)* It's me. Did you guys have a nice Thanksgiving?

ADRIANA. No. *(She whispers.)* He's in a mood.

RHONDA. Well why don't you come to the hospital for a little while? I sent Mike to his parent's house cuz he hasn't spent any time with them and my family already stopped by for "the visit." Drove me crazy the whole time.

ADRIANA. I don't know sweetie. It's late.

RHONDA. Just for a little bit?

ADRIANA. I don't –

RHONDA. Please. Pleeeeaasse??

ADRIANA. Ok. Can I bring you any thing?

RHONDA. Yeah…a mushroom, onion, and olive pizza.

ADRIANA. You got it.

(She hangs up. To audience.) Rhonda has started eating solid food and when she isn't nauseous, which is still most of the time, she gets these cravings. I delight in satisfying them, but often by the time I get to the hospital with her special request, she's nauseous again, so her nurses are the best fed nurses on the floor.

(Lights Shift. It is night time at the hospital. **RHONDA***'s TV is on full blast. We hear an epic soundtrack.)*

RHONDA. Honey come in it already started. Just put it down.

ADRIANA. Don't you want a piece of pizza?

RHONDA. No wait til this scene is over. You know how much I love this part. Sit down.

(to nurse) Gladys what? I told you I don't want to take the pills until after the movie. I'll fall asleep.

(The phone rings.)

Oh my God, it's Grand Central in here today! *(answers phone)* Hello? What? No my parents came by earlier, it was fine. Yeah. No look I gotta go. *Gladiator*'s on. Adriana just walked in with a pizza. I'll talk to you tomorrow. Gotta go – Goodbye!

ADRIANA. He's so hot in that skirt.

RHONDA. He's like an animal. Get him!! Joaquin is such a prick in this. I love him. And he's cute, you know, even with the little scar. Sssssh…What? Gladys, I told you. Not now – goodbye – hurry up Adriana…and action!

*(***RHONDA*** *snaps the imaginary scene chalkboard. Very professional. The two women play out this scene as it appears in the film. It is obvious they have watched it a hundred times.)*

RHONDA. *(as Russell Crowe:)* My name is Gladiator. *(She turns slightly in bed.)*

ADRIANA. *(as Joaquin Phoenix:)* How dare you show your back to me? Slave! You will remove your helmet and tell me your name.

*(***RHONDA*** *mimes taking off her helmet.)*

RHONDA. *(as Russell Crowe:)* My name is Maximus Decimus Meridius. Commander of the armies of the North. General of the Felix – GLADYSSS!!!! Loyal servant to the true Emperor Marcus Aurelius. Father to a murdered son, husband to a murdered wife. I will have my vengeance, in this life, or the next.

(**RHONDA** *puts her helmet back on and grabs the reins of her horse and starts to gallop with her arms.*)

Get him! Get him Adriana!

ADRIANA. I got him. I got him! Ball and chain!

RHONDA. Eye of the tiger!

(**ADRIANA** *lets out a battle cry. As the music swells, she hurls the ball and chain and is victorious!*)

(*Lights shift exuberantly into…*)

ADRIANA. It is two weeks before Valentine's Day and after five eternal months in ICU, Rhonda is now well enough to be moved to the rehab hospital. She can now have living plants and flowers in her room because they are no longer afraid of her dying of an infection. I can't wait to decorate her new room, do a little Feng Shui, make it homey… She tells me that…

RHONDA. This is going to be a very different place. I'm gonna be taking pottery making classes and occupational gardening therapy and the best part is that I'm not going to have to wear this stupid hospital gown anymore. And as soon as I get out of here, we are going to the beach to bring Yemaya her white roses and tell her thank you. I can't wait!

ADRIANA. I am feeling good too! I have been off bread and sugar for three weeks. I am doing my anger work every day, my healing sounds and abdominal massage every other day and I have decided to forgive my parents… so, I'm feelin' good.

I get off the elevator, turn the corner and I see a group of nurses rushing in and out of the room at the end of the hall carrying bloodied dressings. I know that has to be her room. This is a rehab hospital. This is where people come to learn how to walk again. So what the hell is going on down there and why is there so much blood? I just want to turn around and run. I don't have it in me to walk through that door and smile, no matter what I see, again. I don't realize that while I am thinking of a way out, my body has carried me right to her door, until one of the nurses says…

NURSE. *(heavy Korean accent)* Ohhhh you musta be ha friend...Adriana...she expecting you.

ADRIANA. She snaps off her bloody gloves and I think I am going to be sick.

(The lights shift.)

Rhonda's been in rehab now for the past month. Her schedule is so crazy, I have to make an appointment to see her. She barely spends anytime in her room. She is shuttled around to an endless array of therapies, in a wheelchair that costs more than most cars, several times a day. They start the day by strapping her to a tilt board and forcing her to stand upright at varying degrees, for hours, which is excruciating. Then she is shuttled off to the weight room to strengthen her upper body. After that, she is shuttled back up to her room, to have her wounds scraped...to keep activating new skin growth. I am asked to wait outside her door whenever they do this. Her screams are horrifying and I dread being invited back in when it's over.

RHONDA. *(Heavily sedated. Dry mouth. Hands shaking.)* Is this what they saved me for? I can't take any more of this...I wish I had died.

ADRIANA. A rush of reasons of why she should be here... how great she's been doing...how it's a miracle flood my head, but I stop myself from speaking them. I want her to be able to say what she feels and not be talked out of it.

(pause)

I'm glad you're here. I love you.

RHONDA. I feel numb.

(pause)

Will you stay with me until I fall asleep...no one else is coming today.

ADRIANA. *(Hides checking her watch.)* Sure, honey.

RHONDA. Will you give me lovies on my arm?

ADRIANA. Like this?

RHONDA. With your nails...hmmm...Will you tell me a story?

ADRIANA. Ok...uh...I've told you about my Grandmother... well during one of my last visits with her, she was 90, we had just gotten home from seeing Luis Carbonell, the famous Cuban monologist. He recites stories and poems to these intoxicating Cuban rhythms...so Abuela can't stop dancing all around her tiny apartment in Queens....

ABUELA. *(Sings... "La Comparsa")* Mira la que linda viene. Mira la que linda va.... *(She laughs.)*

ADRIANA. Abuela dances over to her altar. Which is an ocean of perfume bottles, each saint had their own fragrance.

RHONDA. Which one was Yemaya's?

ADRIANA. I think it was Tommy Hillfiger. Anyway, I am expecting some kind of an ancestral legacy to be bestowed on me. She hands me a canister of Midnight Musk talcum powder by *Avon*. She swears that it will drive Brian crazy. Apparently she had read in the tea leaves that we weren't doing so well in that department. Then she opens her lingerie drawer, she reaches softly into a sea of silk and takes out a see through scarlet red nightie. She hands it to me with such reverence and says,

ABUELA. Here amor, you enjoy this. Just put this on with a little powder por aqui *(She gestures between her legs.)* y prannn prannn!!

ADRIANA. She boasted that when she'd go for her monthly check ups with her handsome GP, El Doctor Fox, or when she'd make her occasional visits to St. John's Hospital she always put on new lingerie. She claimed that she got better care,

ABUELA. Porque nadie quiere ver una vieja con la narga pa fuera...

ADRIANA. ...because no one wants to see an old lady's ass hanging out. Then she showed me the new nail polish she was going to wear to her next appointment with, El Dr. Fox, called.....

ABUELA. Secretos de Ceresas. De secret of cherries. *(She laughs.)*

ADRIANA. And then she laughed her laugh. The one that felt like a sunset after a long day at the beach. It never occurred to her that she was old or that parts of her body used to live in other places. Better places. It never occurred to her that she wasn't more desirable at 90 then she was at 20. It never occurred to her, so she was.

*(**ADRIANA** fixes **RHONDA**'s blanket and kisses her on the forehead.)*

RHONDA. *(half asleep)* I love you.

ADRIANA. I love you, too. Goodnight.

(to audience) I fill her water glass and say a prayer that she sleeps through the night. I hate leaving her, but these long visits are hard. I mean I go to the hospital with the intention of staying no more than two hours, but something always comes up and I don't know how to leave, so six, seven hours later, I am tired, but as long as I can walk out of that room on two legs...what right do I have to be tired?

ADRIANA. *(on cell phone)* Hey Babe...it's me...pick up...pick up...hello...hello...are you there? *(surprised)* I guess you went out. Baby, look...I...I know I promised we'd spend some time together tonight...Rhonda wasn't doing well and no one else – I just needed to stay...I'm sorry...I – I'm on my way home *(Slams cell phone shut.)*

(Lights shift. Hot Latin beat.)

ESPERANZA. It's nice to make the party. To bring the presents. To bring the glitter. To bring the cha cha. Pero ja nena. Enough. It's time to wake up and smell the doughnuts! When was the last time you had coochie with Brian? Ah? When was the last time you *wanted* coochie? Like Doctor Phil says, ay he's so cute with his little bald head, "How's that working for ju?" Ju remember Mami? In and out...in and out...in in in... out out out...*(She dances off.)*

(Lights shift.)

ADRIANA. *(inspired)* It's mid June and the streets of NY are decorated with smiling young graduates and the fragrance of lilacs and peony from the corner stores. I went on my first audition since 9/11 and I got the part. Parts actually...it's a play...a Calypso version of *The Odyssey.* I play 12 parts in it and rehearsals have been a bitch, but it feels so good to be working again. I've been spending less time at the hospital. I feel bad not being there as much...and...a little relieved to have a legitimate excuse. I am on a break between rehearsing the Helen of Troy scene and the mermaid ménage a trois with Odysseus, he's really cute, when I get a message from Rhonda...

RHONDA. Adriana. I did it. I *walked.* I took 5 steps all by myself. I did it. Can you come by the hospital tomorrow? I want you to see me walk.

ADRIANA. So I go to the hospital early the next morning to see her physical therapy session. I am so excited. I meet her in the therapy room. She wheels in wearing an oversized Bon Jovi t-shirt that one of her doctors had given her from his rocker days and a homemade black wrap skirt...velcroed in the right places. She has state of the art custom made boots, to prevent the bones in her legs from shattering, when she puts her weight on them.

*(As **ADRIANA** recounts this, she re-enacts **RHONDA**'s physical actions simultaneously. **RHONDA**'s movements are slow, sourcing her strength through excruciating pain.)*

Her wheelchair is pulled up between the two parallel bars. Two therapists help her get to her feet. She shakes as she grips fiercely onto the parallel bars... slowly they let go of her. Her torso is hunched way over and I keep waiting for her to straighten up. She draws her right foot out from under her. She inches it forward...right...left. She repeats the motion...right.... left...I notice drops of blood dripping onto the floor... right...left...More blood. Her physical therapist tells her to *stop*...right...left...blood starts gushing...trailing a red path behind her...right...left...right...left... right – her therapists scoop the wheelchair under her, forcing her to stop. *(beat)* I stare at the blood soaked floor. It looks like a murder scene. As they wheel her past me she asks...

RHONDA. *(out of breath, victorious)* Did ya see that? I did it. I walked.

(ADRIANA *tries to share this moment of* RHONDA*'s triumph, but inside it is clear that it is going to be a long time before* RHONDA *will go home.*)

(*Lights shift. We hear a bizarre mambo played on a harpsichord as* ADRIANA *mimes squeezing into a skin tight spandex dress. She hops about throughout the scene as she is unable to move her legs in this dress.*)

ADRIANA. *(excited)* I'm on Tenth Avenue, in my mermaid costume from *The Odyssey* trying to get a cab. I decided to give Rhonda a thrill. I sneaked out the back door of the theater right after the matinee so the stage manager wouldn't see me. I have on a tight green spandex dress that trails a long tail of fishnets and sea shells... I have long green hair...I'm covered in silver glitter. And I'm having a hard time getting a cab! I am rushing to the hospital between shows to help Gabi give Rhonda a facial and do her hair the day before her big magazine interview. I am exhausted, but I know Rhonda's gonna love this. Taxi!

I enter the room and Rhonda and Gabi are deep in

discussion about none other than, Hilary Clinton, who had come to see Rhonda the day before and left her with a mega dose of star fever...Hilary this and Hilary that...

RHONDA. ...and Oh, Gabi, you remind me so much of Hilary. You're always doing something exciting in the world that you believe in and I so admire that. I told her that if she runs for President she can count on my vote – Adriana, what are you wearing?

ADRIANA. My costume from The Odyssey.

RHONDA. Oh. Huh. Anyway, do you want to see the pictures of me and Hilary? She's so much prettier in person. She had on the most beautiful jewelry...

ADRIANA. *(to herself)* Well screw you, Madame. Maybe *Hilary* should be giving you this facial. I am exhausted, on my dinner break, standing here squeezing blackheads and exfoliating ungrateful skin...and not even a *thank you.*

(She squeezes a blackhead out of **RHONDA**'s nose.)

RHONDA. Ow! Adriana what is wrong with you? You're so quiet.

ADRIANA. Nothing, nothing, really. Do you want "Viva Las Vegas" or "Sandcastle" for your nails?
Gabi is making me sick. She is just standing there in her Birkenstocks, acting helpless, while I do all of the work...

(Spoken in a flurry of out of breath effort as she progresses...trying to do it all.)

Can you get me some water? Sure honey. Can you fix my pillows? Of course. Will you massage my arms? Ok. Will you wash my hair? Right away. Will you get me more juice? Absolutely. Will you hand me the phone? You got it. Will you straighten that up? That and more. Will you get me a fresh gown? How bout the pink one? Will you help me put it on? You betcha. Stay for my PT session? I'll coach you on the breathing! Be here when the doctor comes? With a pen and a pad! Stay until I fall asleep? What are friends for?!

(Lights shift. **ESPERANZA***'s Latin beat.)*

ESPERANZA. Ecu me nena, but we hab to talk becuz come dice Whoopi Goldberg in my favorite movie, *Ghost,* "Ju in danger girl!" *(Music fades...)* Ju know it's funny because ju criticize all the fringe friends, but let me tell ju sonsing, they are all a lot smarter than ju, because they all still hab a life. Oh jes they hab a life. Nobody gave up everything for Rhonda. Nobody but ju. An what does that get ju? Tell me? Because who the hell are ju? An what planet did ju fall from to think that ju can make it all better? Pleaaasssse. Been there done that. Let me tell ju sonsing, Ju want to be a goddess? Ju think its jus dancing, eating chocolate, and wearing no panties? *(She lifts her skirt.)* No Mamita...it's work, because ju have to have the courage to *destroy.* Ahh jes...jus as ju have the courage to save, and to birth, and to create, ju have to have the courage to walk away and let sonsing fall. Can ju do that? Can ju walk away and let her fall. Because she has to learn how to e'stand on her own two legs, an if they don't work any more, that's her problem. Not jours. Ju didn't cripple her. And ju can't save her.

(Music returns. **ESPERANZA** *dances off.)*

(Lights shift.)

ADRIANA. Ten months have passed and they have started to significantly decrease the morphine. Rhonda is becoming nasty and unrecognizable. She is now 60 lbs. heavier from all of the medication and her beautifully chiseled face has receded into a bitter and angry scowl. I try to bury myself in the doing, like before, but there is nothing *to do.* I don't even know what to talk about. How do I complain about menstrual cramps, a lousy audition, or the few pounds I gained from the fourth of July BBQ I went to?

I make my way toward Rhonda's bedside to greet her. She scans me from head to toe.

RHONDA. Those pants don't flatter you. Ya gained a little weight?

ADRIANA. I move closer to the door, take a bite of the lunch I brought and say… "Maybe a little."

(*awkward pause*)

RHONDA. Would you hand me my tweezers and my mirror?

(**RHONDA** *proceeds to pluck her eyebrows with shaky hands. She looks up.*)

Are you wearing a bra, cuz from the side your tits look really saggy?

ADRIANA. (*flustered*) No…I'm not wearing a bra.

RHONDA. You know you really shouldn't talk with your mouth full.

ADRIANA. What?

RHONDA. I said you shouldn't talk with your mouth full. It's disgusting.

ADRIANA. Disgusting?

RHONDA. Yeah. That's what I said. Disgusting. Hand me my water –

(*loaded pause…*)

(**ADRIANA** *pours a glass of water.*)

ADRIANA. I hand Rhonda her water, I close my mouth, and I chew. I chew my rage. I chew my hurt. I chew my hope of how I couldn't wait 'til they took her off the heavy drugs because, as I understood it, that meant that more of Rhonda was going to come back. Right? That's what the doctors kept saying…more of her was going to come back…

I can't do this. I can't. I don't know how to be in a room with her any more, or home with Brian, or anywhere. I mean I was ready for a sprint. You know? Drop everything because Rhonda might die – no she's going to be ok – no she might die – gotta get down there – no she's ok – no she's might die…run-run-run!!! Well I've dropped everything for the past year and even though she's not going to die anymore, I don't know how to pick it all back up.

I need a break...please. I just need a break...to catch
my breath...and then...maybe...I can come back and
bring something in the room that's alive again.

So I tell Rhonda that I need to take a couple of weeks
off. Okay, I can't bring myself to say that to her face, so
I write it in a card. A beautiful hand-painted card with
mermaids and unicorns on it. I tell her that I love her
and that I have some things I need to work out, and
when I don't hear from her, I think she is ok with it.

A couple of weeks pass. *(Catches herself.)* Okay, six weeks
pass and I am feeling better. Gabi and I are having
lunch. She has been spending more time with Rhonda
and I appreciate the updates. We are at my favorite Greek place, Nikos, and somewhere between the
hummus and the spanakopita she says...

GABRIELLA. Rhonda's getting out of the hospital tomorrow.

ADRIANA. What?

GABRIELLA. Yeah. She's going home tomorrow.

ADRIANA. Why didn't she tell me?

GABRIELLA. She doesn't want you to know.

(**ADRIANA** *is speechless.*)

GABRIELLA. I know it's just her pride talking. Look there's
going to be a party for her and some TV show is going
to be there to film it. We're all going and I think you
should go too.

(**ADRIANA** *shakes her head in disbelief.*)

GABRIELLA. Adriana, she's hurt. She says you just walked
out on her.

ADRIANA. And what did you say? *(Silence.* **ADRIANA** *slams
down her money)* That should cover my share.
I walk out of the restaurant pounding my feet into the
pavement down Broadway. I can't believe she doesn't
want me there. What kind of bullshit is that? I bet all
the little feel good fringe friends will be there right?
Funny how when the TV cameras are there people
manage to show up!

Fine. I'm not even going to watch it. What am I going to see? These jack asses smiling while the TV show milks the moment of her "loyal friends" all around her. Makes me sick. Why don't they show her screaming and smelling and looking like a witch on TV? Huh? Why don't they let America see what that looks like. No let's just see the pretty picture of the crippled girl going home.

I should just go down there right now and say you know what bitch? I'm here. You can't get rid of me with your little sleeping beauty act. That's right the wicked fairy is here.

Taxi!

NURSE. Excuse me...

ADRIANA. The head nurse says....

NURSE. You're not allowed to go in there.

ADRIANA. *(ridiculously kind)* Oh no...don't worry, she's expecting me. *(to Audience)* I walk into Rhonda's room and she's sitting there like the Queen of Sheba, eating ice cream, and watching *Survivor...*

(to **RHONDA***)*

So you don't want me to know you're getting out of the hospital tomorrow huh? What kind of bullshit is that?

RHONDA. I've got nothing to say to you. Get out of my room.

ADRIANA. No, I'll get out of here when I say what I came here to say. Now, you tell all these morons that haven't been here to come and share this day with you, this day that we have dreamed about for a fucking year and shhhh don't tell Adriana because I don't want her there. How ungrateful can you possibly be?

RHONDA. How ungrateful? Adriana, you just checked out. You walk out on me, I have no idea what's going on. You send me a stupid little card and you expect me to be fine with that? Well, I'm not fine with that. And since you've been gone *other* people have been here and they've been good to me.

ADRIANA. So six weeks cancels out a year of me being here? Where were all your little migratory birds then huh? I was here when every fuckin' body wasn't. Alright, Mike was here, I'll pardon him, he did his best. But every one else came when it was *convenient*, when they could squeeze you in. Do you know the things I've put on hold to be here with you?!

RHONDA. Lower your voice. You're makin' me sick. I didn't ask you to make me your little patient. I didn't ask you to try to save me, I had doctors for that! I thought you were here because you love me, but obviously you had other reasons for being here.

ADRIANA. What? Have the drugs left you with amnesia with a capital A? Who was by your bedside when your life was hanging in the balance, praying over your body, putting talismans and charms in your room, calling in supernatural help so you'd survive? Who loved you and fed you and caressed you when these so called other *friends* were too scared to come in here and see you near death, or smell your shit, or listen to you scream?? I was here and I know you're alive because of me.

RHONDA. Nobody saved me...and the reason why I am getting out of this hospital tomorrow is because of me. I'm the one that got myself up every morning. I'm the one who stood on these two legs no matter how much it hurt, no matter how much I was bleeding. I'm the one who did the work to get the hell out of this hospital and get the hell out of this bed, so don't you try to pretend that you had anything to do with that because you know what? I saved myself! Now get the hell out of my room. I don't want you here.

   (pause)

ADRIANA. I never had that conversation with Rhonda. The taxi never made it to the hospital. Instead and I don't know why, I got out of the cab at Ground Zero.

   (Lights shift slowly as beautiful music plays very softly... supporting this moment without being sentimental.)

I get out and walk all the way up to the footprints of the Towers. All the way up to the makeshift fence surrounding the quiet earth. Space. So much space. This hole...this empty tomb...I am standing there pressed up to the fence just taking it all in, when some idiot tourist pushes me out of the way, *(Music ends.)* so that he and his oblivious little group have more room to take their picture. They are all just standing there grinning like they are in Times Square on New Years Eve.

And then I see them. Double-decker buses. Tourists disembarking, disembarking to cross the street and stand in front of the gated fence and take pictures at Ground Zero like they are standing in front of the Statue of Liberty or the Empire State Building and they're all smiling. And to the right of them is a vendor, with a little program that has the Towers burning on the cover and it says "Day of Tragedy"...5 dollars. Day of Tragedy...5 dollars. Day of Tragedy...5 dollars??? Next to the souvenir program are neat little stacks of "I've been to Ground Zero" t-shirts in small, medium, and extra large. I want to know what you do with a t-shirt from Ground Zero. I want to know what the hell that means, because I don't understand how it is that in our country we don't have a way for people to mourn...like do you remember after it happened, St. Paul's church right across the street from Ground Zero had that fence that went all the way around four city blocks and people spontaneously came down here with their flowers, t-shirts, cards, their candles...stuffed animals and rosaries...baseball hats...symbols that meant something to them, whether they were people who knew some one that was lost, or just a stranger coming here from some far away place, because they had to. I mean how did we get from that to...Day of Tragedy...5 dollars...

I march right up to the Grey Line Bus and I yell...

"Do you know where you are? And what the fuck are you smiling at?"

I stand in front of the fence rooting myself into the wounded earth, determined to stay here and prevent any more idiots from smiling, when I hear a voice say…

EDDIE. *(older Puerto Rican man)* It's ok, Mama. They don't understand.

ADRIANA. I look to my left and standing there is my own white-haired, Puerto Rican version of Clarence, from, *It's a Wonderful Life.* He has on a wide-brimmed Panama hat, a starched white linen guayabera and a smile as open as the sea. He hands me his sandalwood scented handkerchief and says…

EDDIE. I come here every day.

ADRIANA. He takes a beat up old camera out of his shirt pocket, he kisses it and says…

EDDIE. This will be with me until the day I die. Can I show you sonsing?

ADRIANA. He takes some pictures out of a worn envelope.

EDDIE. I almost died that day. I was e'standing right here when the towers was burning. I took these pictures while I was trying to get away. I was choked by the black smoke when the building collapse…I was trying to get away. That's all I can remember until I woke up inside di ambulance and dis big strong young Latino man was punching me in the chest saying…

"C'mon Papi. C'mon Papi. You're not going to die on me. You breathe. C'mon Papi. C'mon. Breathe. Breathe." And as I was watching him, I thought he was my son. I don't have a son, but if I had one, I thought, that's what he would look like.

And all of a sudden, I e'start to breathe.

And my new son scream, "You're alive Papi! You're alive!"

And I was alive!

So I looked him up a few weeks later because I wanted to tell him thank you. And you know what he say to me, "No Papi, thank you. You're my hero, because the one life that I was able to save that day….yours….somehow helps me get through all this."

ADRIANA. I am still holding onto his handkerchief when he asks…

EDDIE. Would it be ok if I take your picture?

(**ADRIANA** *nods.*)

EDDIE. *(He raises the camera up to his eye.)* And it's okay if ju e'smile.

(Camera flash. Lights shift. **ADRIANA** *moves about the stage as she composes the letter.)*

ADRIANA. Dear Rhonda, I'm still so hurt that you…
Dear Rhonda, I think this silence between us is…
Dear Rhonda, I wish that we could…

Dear Rhonda, I know it has been more than seven years since we last spoke. I have filled many notebooks trying to write this letter. I'm sure a lot has changed for us both. Brian and I broke up. I left New York for LA, and I learned how to drive, which we know is a big deal for a New Yorker. I go to the beach every so often to bring Yemaya her white roses and thank her. I say a prayer that you are ok. I shave my legs regularly now. I remember how it used to drive you crazy when I didn't. But no bikini waxing. I've fired myself from my full time job of trying to save the people I love because I know that I can't. I wanted so much to give you everything I could, but I didn't know how to do that, and keep some for myself. I didn't know and nobody around me knew…they all kept saying, you just need to get back to "normal." And what the hell was that? Normal. I kept putting myself in your bed and doing what I thought I would want someone to do for me. But you never asked me for that. I fucked up Rhonda, I was too much of a coward to tell you what I was feeling and what I needed when things started to fall apart. I didn't know how, and I didn't try. I listened to the "experts" who said not to bring anything emotionally upsetting into your room. So I didn't. I am so sorry that it looked like I walked out on you. That's not what happened. I was shocked and hurt when you shut me out….but the gift…

What I learned… is that love isn't doing, love is being… being real, being myself, and that my heart, which I have spent most of my life protecting, is the strongest muscle I have in my body, and every time I use it, it just get stronger...so Rhonda, I am willing to give up the anger and the hurt, the questions, and my need to be right...the fear....because when I do... what is left is love. I love you. And I can't help but wonder what it would be like to bump into you somewhere...and have the chance to just look into each other's eyes... you know...like on a street corner, or on the subway, or...or on an airplane...

(Lights shift. Some magic.)

ADRIANA. *(cont)*...first class...I am sinking into the large leather seats, resting against the large down pillow, wondering why the windows are the same size as coach. I look fabulous...I'm wearing...uhh...BCBG... and I am listening to ABBA's greatest hits on my headphones...I look up and see you, dressed to the nines, looking gorgeous. You walk down the aisle and take the seat next to me...I take a deep breath and I say...

(To RHONDA.*)* Hi.

RHONDA. Hello. *(She looks her up and down.)* BCBG. *(*ADRIANA *smiles.)* You changed your hair.

ADRIANA. I did.

RHONDA. Looks nice.

ADRIANA. Thanks. I hold the left ear piece of my headphones up to your ear and slowly, as if against your better judgment, you accept it.

*(*ADRIANA *starts to sing* Dancing Queen *gently to* RHONDA...*tentative,* RHONDA *joins her...gradually they grow to full girlfriend volume.* We hear the plane's engine revving up as it starts to race down runway.* ADRIANA *grabs* RHONDA*'s hand. Music swells as the plane lifts off into the sky.)*

Lights fade to black.

End of Play

From the Reviews of
TAKING FLIGHT...

"Brave Lady. Brave Tale. Brave Performance."
- Daily News

"...Enthralling play...Sevahn-Nichols is a remarkable actor and storyteller. She flows seamlessly between portraying herself and the other character...Her strong charisma and her ability to keep the pace fast without feeling rushed are impressive. The tightly written script is honest and unafraid to jump radically from dark moments to humorous ones. The play is ultimately about not giving up...a celebration of life...and an example of how good a one person show can be. Kirk Douglas came onstage and praised her talent and her bravery. He was right on both accounts."
- Back Stage

" Adriana Sevahn-Nichols...is an energetic, endearing, enthusiastic, intriguing writer and performer. She craftily mixes comedy with tragedy...using the art and power of the spoken word. Out of it comes a message for mourners as well as survivors."
- Hollywood Reporter

"An inviting character study with a cinematic air...has all the earmarks of a Hollywood chic pic, but pays dividends in the theatre through rich description and exacting language. This work has a healthy life ahead of it."
- Variety

"...Spinning a thought-provoking tale out of diverse autobiographical threads...*Taking Flight* bears witness to the way personal struggle connects to larger public conflict."
- Los Angeles Times

OTHER TITLES AVAILABLE FROM SAMUEL FRENCH

...AND BABY MAKES TWO – an adoption tale

Nanci Christopher

Dramatic Comedy / 1f

A single woman's desire to experience motherhood without a husband at her side sends her through the world of adoption. Her path leads her through an array of characters and situations rife with drama. Settling on private adoption through an attorney she suffers an unfathomable heartbreak at the death of her newborn son. She is somehow able to rise out of despair to try again and meets Elizabeth who is looking for someone to adopt her unborn child. A new family is forged through the courage of two very brave women.

The running time is one hour.

"Christopher's messages about love and following your dreams are worth telling...fascinating material."
- *Back Stage West*

...AND BABY MAKES TWO – an adoption tale was nominated for the 2009 SUSAN SMITH BLACKBURN PRIZE.

OTHER TITLES AVAILABLE FROM SAMUEL FRENCH

THE YEAR OF MAGICAL THINKING

Joan Didion

Drama / 1f
"This happened on December 30, 2003. That may seem a while ago but it won't when it happens to you . . ."

In this dramatic adaptation of her award-winning, bestselling memoir (which *The New York Times* called "an indelible portrait of loss and grief...a haunting portrait of a four-decade-long marriage), Joan Didion transforms the story of the sudden and unexpected loss of her husband and their only daughter into a stunning and powerful one-woman play.

The Broadway production of *The Year of Magical Thinking* opened at the Booth Theatre on March 29, 2007, starring Vanessa Redgrave and directed by David Hare.

Joan Didion was born in California and lives in New York City. She is the author of five novels and seven previous books of nonfiction.

CPSIA information can be obtained at www.ICGtesting.com
Printed in the USA
BVOW11s0806260214

346063BV00010B/391/P